# ❧HOW TO TRAIN YOUR OWNER❧

By

## Anna, the Golden Labrador

with a little help from

## Mike Gibb

Foreword by Michelle McManus

All illustrations by David Stout of Sketchpad

*All Best wishes.*

*Anna + Mike Gibb*

© Hame Press 2013

By the same Authors

**Anna, the Golden Labrador**

*Ask Anna (An A to Z Guide For Dogs)*

**Mike Gibb**

Books

*It's A Dawgs Life*
*Waiting For The Master*
*Ask Anna (An A to Z Guide For Dogs)*

Musical Plays

*A Land Fit For Heroes*
*Mother of All the Peoples*
*Five Pound & Twa Bairns*
*Sunday Mornings On Dundee Law*
*Clarinda*
*Outlander*
*Red Harlaw*
*Aberdeen's Forgotten Diva*
*Just Another Seterday*

Plays

*Children Of The Sea*
*Lest We Forget*
*Doorways In Drumorty*

This book is dedicated

to all the thousands of animals

who have passed through the Bianca shelter

and whose lives have been saved by

the dedication of a small band of very special people

*"Rescuing one dog will not change the world.*

*But it will change the world for that one dog."*

Always wanted to eat the same food as your humans? Well now you can with new improved

# DEDGEEGEE CHUM

Made with genuine horsemeat just like hamburgers, lasagne and other foods bought by humans from leading supermarkets

Make Dedgeegee Chum your stable diet

I first had the pleasure of meeting Anna the Labrador and her master Mike Gibb back in 2009 when they both appeared on STV's The Hour to promote their book 'Ask Anna'. I immediately connected with them as I have always been a huge animal lover especially when it comes to dogs because of a very special little lady who came into my life back in the summer of 1995. I was 15yrs old and living at home with my wonderful parents and four sisters. It was during the summer holidays when my younger sister Laura came running through the front door shouting "Mum, Mum you have to come round to the pet shop immediately. Someone has handed in a bag of puppies and if they don't find a home tonight the man in the pet shop said he can't keep them".

You see earlier that day the owner of the pet shop had rescued a box of 3 week old mongrel puppies and was desperately trying to find homes for them all that night because they needed round the clock care and lots of TLC having been unfortunately separated from their mother at such a young age. My own mother dismissed the idea at first as our house was already fit to burst with seven people under its roof but after much pleading and begging from us all she eventually gave in and went to the pet shop.

Almost one hour later she returned with the most gorgeous tiny wee bundle you have ever seen. Curled up in the palm of her hand was a little black puppy with four white paws, a white tummy, a white tip on the end of her tail and a little white stripe down her nose. She was just perfect and we named her Bonnie on the count of her being so beautiful. Bonnie was the most wonderful dog a person could wish to have and she brought so much love and happiness to our home for 15 unforgettable years until she sadly passed away in October 2010. I was with her until the very end along with my father and mother and we took great comfort that she was surrounded by the people who loved her all her life and it was our way of saying thank you to her for all of the love and happiness she brought to our family.

I am honoured to have the privilege of sharing my story with you because Bonnie McManus certainly trained her humans to love and understand her and I hope that with all the proceeds from the sale of this book, many many more animals will have the chance to do the same.

*Michelle McManus*

Dear Reader,

I honestly don't know how often over the last three years a fellow canine has come up to me when I have been out walking and without even bothering to greet me in the traditional way (sniffing my butt) has blurted out, "when are you going to write a follow up to *Ask Anna?*". Let's just say that if I had a dog treat for every time that has happened, I would be a very portly Labrador indeed.

Well, here is the good news. The long wait is over.

I don't want you thinking that the delay was because the fame and fortune (not that there was any of that; without a bye your leave, the "master" insisted on giving it all to charity – makes him feel good or something) had gone to my head. Okay, what girl wouldn't be affected by having her photo plastered over newspapers, local and national, and chatting to Michelle on *The Hour?*\*.

But no, that wasn't the problem. I guess in music industry parlance, as Mick\*\* said to me one day, it all comes down to that difficult second album. If you produce something as ground breaking as *Ask Anna* you don't want to turn out anything that doesn't match up. And for so long I just couldn't think of a suitable subject.

And then one day on a walk in the park (which writing this book certainly hasn't been) it came to me. I was watching a family with a dog and couldn't believe how badly trained all the humans were. I thought to myself "if only there were training classes for dog owners"; after all we are knee deep in classes designed to train dogs, all under the guidance of people that in a previous life were clearly guards in a Siberian Gulag and who are somehow able to convince fellow humans that they "understand dogs". Aye, in their dreams.

I knew I couldn't actually start such a class – I mean where would we hold it? I'm certainly not having a bunch of strangers tramping around my abode. But then it came to me in a flash of genius (yup yet another one) - I could write a book on the subject. The shelves in your local Waterstones groan under the weight of tomes on the subject of dog training. And yes, I do speak from personal experience. I know dogs are not allowed into book shops. But "dog authors" are. Na nana nana. So I know for a fact that the section on training dog owners is rather sparse. Indeed the total number of such books is a nice round number. Zero.

And let's face it, no one is better equipped to undertake such a task than me. After all, I am not only an author of some repute but I have many, many years of experience in the training of humans. And believe me, if my "Mr & Mrs" can be trained, anyone can.

Along the way I have added a bit of humour, a guide to things a dog should and shouldn't do and have even let my co-author pitch in with a few true stories. I am sure you all know "how lucky you are". Let's face it, probably not a day goes by that you aren't told that. But in truth when you read some of these tales of life in a shelter in a far off land, you begin to realise that perhaps we are not quite as hard done by as we may think we are.

And if all that wasn't enough, (personally I think it is far too much for the modest price you paid for this book) I have even included a section on cooking and baking for dogs, with recipes provided by my Aunt Heather from Kitchener (isn't that a great place for a cook to come from?) in Canada. Now she isn't my "real Aunt" (don't even go down that biological route – I never knew any of my Aunts, but that's a long and painful story and one that I have no intention of sharing here).

No I call her Aunt Heather because she's a great baker (her Bernie's Bianca Biscuits are to die for ***) and she reminds me of the woman who makes all those yummy pancake mixes and syrups and the like, Aunt Jemima. Except that Aunt Heather isn't fat. Nor does she have black hair (Aunt Heather might have had one day; but now its night). Nor does she look remotely like Oprah Winfrey. Otherwise, she's a dead ringer for her.

Anyway all of these wonders are crammed into this little volume. So put your paws up and prepare to enter the wonderful world of owner training.


*Anna Gibb, Author*

*I wish to make it abundantly clear that the subsequent demise of this little show had nothing whatsoever to do with my appearance on it.

**What do you mean "name dropper"? I'm taking about Mick, the nice guy who empties the buckets and sweeps up in my local park, not that old wrinkly, decrepit geezer who refuses to stop singing about getting off of his cloud or something.

***Not be taken literally. It's just one of those silly things humans say.

# ☙ TRAIN YOUR OWNER TO ☙
# SIT & STAY

I have started with this subject not because it is hugely important or difficult but quite simply because it is invariably the first section on any "How to Train your Dog" book. But why?

What is this obsession that humans have with getting their dog to sit? Take for example going for a walk on the lead. If your human has trained you, (and my pair fortunately knew better than to even try) you will no doubt come to the end of the pavement and prepare to cross the road. So what do they get you to do? Sit. Again I ask why?

It's not as if dogs have been designed with rubber bottoms so they can bounce over the road is it? So you sit and wait and then they get you to stand again so you can walk over the road. Pointless or what?

And it's not just outside. If they are going to give you a treat they will invariably begin with the command "sit". Now I am not an expert on medical matters (one of the few disciplines I haven't mastered if truth be told) but I am pretty sure that the dog's digestive system hasn't been designed to make it easier to process food when sitting down; quite the contrary I would assume, bearing in mind that I have never known a dog that sits down to eat his plate of food.

And it's not just "sit". What about "stay"? When they are training you they will invariably get you to sit and then walk away as far as possible before telling you "come". Does that make any sense to you? Thought not. Why didn't you just accompany them in the first place and avoid all that palaver.

No doubt some philosopher came up with some "wise" statement about everything having a purpose or something*. So on that basis, I set to work trying to solve this little conundrum and I eventually cracked it.

Owners teach their dogs to "sit" and "stay" for no other reason than to show that they are the boss (stop laughing – they really believe they are) and so they can display to everyone just how clever they are. I'm sure you've seen that smug look on your owner's face after YOU have done something clever.

But this is not a book about dog training; quite the opposite in fact so let's gets started. And we'll begin with "sit". To be brutally honest, you won't have much trouble in getting your humans to sit. Training them to move again is a much more challenging task. Certainly in our house "he" has mastered sitting and spends most of every day doing just that. Okay, okay he does take me for a couple of decent walks every day (oh dear, I've just bitten my tongue) but for the rest of the day he sits to eat, he sits to watch the T.V. and he sits at the computer. Oh boy, does he ever. What he gets to do day after day I don't know but if anyone is ever looking for him, (truthfully only the "little darlings"** are ever likely to give a monkeys where he is) you'll find him staring at the computer screen.

On the other hand, "she" seldom sits down as she constantly finds something that needs cleaning. How could the house always need cleaned I hear you ask? And for once yours truly is stumped for an answer. I mean it's not like I bring any dirt into the house is it?

And if she isn't cleaning, she's ironing or washing things or cooking or something similar. But then, just like someone has flipped a switch, she suddenly sits down and anything less than an earthquake measuring 7.8 on the Richter scale won't get her to move.

This sudden and remarkable change in the creature's habits is simply explained***. It coincides with the arrival of the local "newspaper", the Evening Express which "her indoors" devours, every single day, from cover to cover. Or almost from cover to cover.

She starts, naturally, with the big news on the front page. Sensational stories like, "Vandals set fire to pensioner's wheelie bin" and "City park gets a new swing". Obviously that level of ground breaking stories can't be maintained, but undeterred "she" ploughs on regardless, page after exciting page (although I suspect she rather skips over the one page**** devoted to world news i.e. anything that has happened out with a fifty mile radius of Aberdeen).

She even reads the "letters to the Editor" page despite the fact that, judging by the standard of literacy, most of them have

13

been written in crayon, and that they invariably plough the same old furrow:

*I was in my local park the other day and couldn't believe how much dog mess there was blah, blah, blah" Mrs I.A.M. Moaner, Queens Road.*

And then suddenly, five pages from the back of the paper she stops, totally ignoring that final section, devoted to sports coverage (which coincidentally is the only part of the paper that "he" ever looks at). So does she then put it down? Not on your Nellie she doesn't.

Back she goes to the Sudoku puzzles and from there it is the classified advertisements, which she insists in studying in great detail. Why I don't know; after all, she is not likely to be interested in a lightweight fishing rod when she doesn't fish or a set of conservatory furniture when there isn't a glorified green house for humans at her house or a set of wheel discs for a VW Polo when I am sure she never has or never will own one. But nevertheless, she reads them religiously every day. There was a time when I used to be concerned when I saw her reading the "Dogs for sale" ads. After all, I am the King in this particular Canine Castle and I have no intention of sharing that distinction with any other dog.

Eventually, however, it dawned on me. To her the Classified Advertisements are what Everest is to an accomplished mountaineer, a sort of "If you print them, she will read".

And then finally she arrives at the Death Announcements which she studies diligently. It doesn't seem to matter to her that she has never met 99.9% of the people who have snuffed it. And let's face it, if she hasn't met them before they get their name check in the paper, the chances of her bumping into them thereafter are pretty low. Still, every night she reads them all.

So we have established that there is really no need to train your human to "sit" and that pretty much applies to the command "stay" as well. In our house, all he needs is a computer screen and all she needs is an evening newspaper and I suspect that something similar probably applies in your domicile. However, there has been a little "discussion" ongoing between him and her in recent times about her alleged inability to "stay" in a supermarket.

I bemoan elsewhere in this book the way authorities preclude dogs from going into supermarkets so as a result all this information has been gleaned purely from eavesdropping from the back of the car, while nonchalantly peering out the window and adopting an air of indifference, as they return from a shopping trip. Listening in to what could best be described as a "lively" conversation.

I probably shouldn't tell you about this but I know I can count on your discretion and not pass it onto anyone else (unless of course you can exchange it for a juicy piece of gossip in which case I totally understand). Anyway, it seems that while shopping, "her indoors" has got into a habit of disappearing just as they begin paying, leaving "him" to do all the packing himself before she returns with one, probably unnecessary, item just at the very moment that the last of the shopping has been rung up. This mucks up the till, upsets the cashier and causes "him" no end of embarrassment.

For this reason "he" has apparently started on a course of training "her" to "stay". Chances of success? To my mind pretty slim*****

But this book is not concerned with minor domestic disputes among our owners, but rather about how to train them to do what we dogs want them to do. So without further ado let's get on with it.


*Surely you don't expect word for word philosopher quotes for a fiver

**there will be undoubtedly a lot of mentions of the "little darlings" in this book. In truth, I think the granddaughters are okay and we have a pretty decent mutual respect. No, the problem is with "him and her" and the fact that in their rose tinted eyes the girls can never do anything wrong.

***this line will be more effective if you imagine it being delivered in David Attenborough's hushed tones

****Yes, one whole page

*****Slim = a palm sized sphere of white frozen water in Satan's fiery abode

# 🐾 TRAIN YOUR OWNER TO 🐾 FETCH

I know you will be amazed to discover that the simple task of "Fetching" might prove a problem for humans but sadly that is the case. After all, even the dimmest pampered pedigree pooch can grasp the idea of fetching and retrieving an object in a couple of days (assuming you can manage to get your owner to maintain their concentration for that length of time) provided an adequate supply of tasty treats is proffered in return for our display of intelligence.

As you know we are happy to perform the task irrespective of the size or shape of the object hurled; let's face it, we are just as pleased to chase a cheap tennis ball (three in a pack from Poundland – just remember and tell them Anna sent you) as some fancy shaped piece of plastic "amusingly" (and I use that word in the loosest possible sense) shaped like a hot dog or a bone with a squeaker that is officially guaranteed to survive no more than five minutes of gentle chewing. And, of course, when Christmas rolls around, we all end up chasing after little plastic Santas, don't we? Hilarious isn't it? Still, if they want to believe in Santa who are we to spoil their fun and to point out that the only person likely to enter their house carrying a large sack on a dark December night is someone who has skipped off community service and wants to avail himself of a 52" flat screen smart T.V. without all that bother of having to go to Currys.

So if fetching comes so naturally to us why is it so difficult to train our owners to do it? Well first off I should explain that it isn't as major an issue as you might envisage as 50% of the human population have no trouble with the concept. The "hers". No, the problem lies solely with the male of the species.

Send a female out shopping and she will return with everything on her list plus loads more that she didn't realise she needed until she came across it as she relentlessly pounded the aisles of the supermarket. Only problem is that it does take her several hours.

So how can it take so long I hear you ask?

I'll try and explain. Let's assume that one of the items on her copious list is a packet of digestive* biscuits. So what does she do? Walks along the biscuit aisle, picks up a packet, puts it in her trolley and moves on. Right? Wrong, totally wrong. This process involves several quite complicated steps:

*Step1. Examine every single different make of digestive biscuits and compare the prices.*

Now if they were all the same size of pack that would be a relatively simple task. But in fact, some will contain more biscuits than others so she needs to spend a considerable time working out which is the best value taking account of both price and weight.

*Step 2. Check if they come in multi packs.*

If so, she has to work out if it is cheaper to buy that multi pack rather than two single packs of the same biscuit. Or another brand. And so on.

*Step 3. Check out the reduced section.*

If you thought that stage three would simply involve placing the chosen packet (or multi pack) into the trolley and moving on, you would be quite wrong. It does involve moving but only along the aisle to the section where they place all the reduced items, the ones with bright yellow tickets that "her indoors" sits in the car and peels off before she gets home in case someone would think she is a cheapskate. As if! You would easily recognise this part of the supermarket if the Gestapo that run this country would follow our intelligent European neighbours and let dogs into a shop, but from what I am told, it's the place that several women crowd around, discreetly elbowing each other out of the way to try to get at the bargains.

*Step 4. Check if the reduced pack is cheaper.*

Now life is simple for her if there are no digestives on the reduced shelves. She will simply go back and get the chosen pack (or multi pack). However, if there is a packet of digestives with the telling yellow sticker, then it has to be carried back to the main display where the complicated process of working out if the reduced biscuits of a certain brand are really a better buy than the full price ones of another brand takes place.

19

*Step 5. Chose a packet of digestives.*

For the sake of simplicity, let's assume that the bargain bin didn't come up trumps, then you would expect her to place a packet of the chosen digestives in the trolley and to move on to another part of the shop wouldn't you? Well, not quite. The sell by dates have to be checked first. It doesn't matter that, bearing in mind the speed she eats them at, they will be finished in days not the months that the most recent sell by date allows. She has to get the one with the "best date".

Finished? Nearly. She does take a packet of the digestives but only after, with considerable difficulty and a display of dexterity that could just about get her a trial for the local gymnastics team, she has reached for one at the very back of the display. Why I hear you ask? Because all the packets at the front have been handled.

Mainly by her.

Now if you multiply this procedure by every item on her shopping list, it is not hard to see why it takes so long to accomplish this fetching task. But at least she eventually does.

Not so "him". If he is sent out to fetch he invariably returns, relatively quickly, but with practically nothing on the list he was given. So what goes wrong?

The problem is that the average human male shops under duress (no, it's not a place!) and can't maintain sufficient interest for long enough to complete the task. Even when they are sent out by her with a neatly written list of what is needed, the exercise invariably ends up in abject failure.

You see it is most unusual for both the list and "him" to arrive simultaneously at the supermarket. Sure he gets there but the list is more than likely still on the kitchen table where she placed it for him or in the hall where he laid it down to pick up his car keys or in the pocket of a pair of trousers he changed out of just before he left the house or in his car or in a dozen other places. Where it seldom if ever is, is in his hand.

So he enters the shop, listless**, desperately trying to remember what was on it and is doing not too badly until he arrives at the newspaper stand, picks up a paper and then that's that. The next twenty minutes are spent aimlessly wandering around the shop while catching up on the day's news; not the boring stuff on the front page but the latest happenings down Govan way and all thoughts of why he is in the Supermarket are quickly replaced by the blissful feeling engendered by the latest misfortunes to afflict Rangers F.C.

Half an hour later he's home with six cans of Carlsberg, two super size packs of Pringles (that were on special offer), a large meat feast pizza, a pack of diced best steak only suitable for a slow cooker (which they don't own) and, of course, a Daily Record. None of which appeared on the list which he finds on his return, sitting under the gloves which he decided at the last minute he didn't need. And so it's a night in the dog house*** for him.

21

So why should this be of any concern to us I hear you enquire? Because my little canine pals, the famous missing list contained six cans of Butcher tripe and a pack of rawhide chews. So if you don't want to end up being served a plate of dried food with the words "sorry darling, Daddy forgot to get your tinned food" you better start training him to fetch.

So how do you do that? Well obviously you can't simply reverse the human/dog method. "He" is hardly likely to scurry across the room for the simple promise of a dog treat is he? In truth I've never seen him scurry; well except to get out of the room if certain people come on the T.V.****.

No, what you need to do is to teach him the benefit of putting something where it can be easily found again. And hopefully, once he has been trained to do that with something he cares about, he will apply the same principle to the likes of a shopping list.

The first step is to think of something that is important to the average man. In truth it comes down to two items – a can of beer and the TV remote control. There is a third, but he probably keeps the Ann Summers catalogue on a high shelf you can't reach.

Which one to choose? Well the can of beer has obvious disadvantages. It is difficult for a dog to lift and there is a real danger of piercing the metal with your teeth and tasting the stuff. It certainly looks disgusting, all frothy, and I'm told it tastes even worse and leaves you with disgusting breath that smells like...like...his.

In that case there really is only one choice. The T.V. remote. While a television set in a shop may appear to belong to a Mr. Samsung or a Mr. Sony, the moment it enters the family home it becomes his and his only and he guards the all important remote control with his life.

So all you need to do is pick it up and hide it. Simple? Well, yes and no. You have to make sure you don't make it too easy to find or he'll never get the message. But on the other hand, don't make it too difficult either. If you do there is a real danger of him giving up (humans have little staying power) and start reading a paper he has picked up somewhere along the way, quite forgetting what he was originally doing. On top of that, if you hide it too well he'll start blaming "her" for moving it. In truth that's the very first thing he'll do on the basis that it was ABH's ***** fault. But if the search goes on too long things might get a little less than agreeable in the home and the romantic meal with wine planned for later (which often involves you joining in courtesy of a decent treat one of them has bought) will most certainly be off.

So how long will it take before he gets the message? How long is a piece of string?****** Every "he" is different and in truth you will just have to carry on with the little experiment under the penny drops.

If you are stuck with a particularly thick and difficult human male, just remember that giving up too soon could result in you ending up eating dried food that would make the even average couscous meal look appetizing.

23

*similar to Bonios except they taste of something

**no, not tired; devoid of list

***I don't know why they say this. Do you know of any fellow canine that sleeps in a dog house? If you do, please pass on my condolences.

**** Lenny Henry, Brian Blessed, Paul Daniels, Graham Norton, Miranda Hart, everyone from every Scottish "comedy" sit com ever made, Lenny Henry (he is worth mentioning twice), Sandi Toskvig, Russell Howard and...well, in truth, basically anyone who is not in a Danish series.

*****Anyone But Him

******60 metres if bought in Tesco

# Stories from the Shelter

## RENE

It was another warm, sleepy day in Portugal when one of the volunteers from the Bianca shelter decided to spend sometime relaxing on one of the many quiet, secluded beaches near Sesimbra. That decision had remarkable consequences for one little dog; in truth it was a life saver.

As the volunteer lay on the sand enjoying the sun rays, she became aware of three people, a man and two women, crossing the beach and something about their demeanour seemed odd and made her sit up and take notice. And as she watched, she noticed that one of them was carrying a bag. Not unusual on a beach where people bring their swimwear and a towel. Except for the fact that this bag was moving as if something inside was trying to get out. Desperately trying to get out.

As she continued to watch, the content of the bag was dumped on the beach and then covered with an old flannel shirt onto which sand was heaped. Having completed their task the trio scurried off. Not surprisingly, the volunteer decided to investigate and was horrified by what she found.

For once she had removed the sand and the shirt she found herself staring at a small, very dirty and very distressed little dog. A dog that had been abandoned on that beach to suffer a slow and painful death.

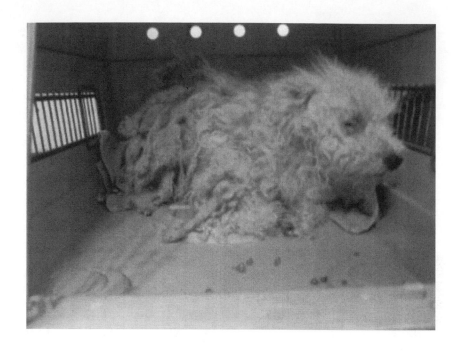

It was impossible to tell what sort of dog it was. One thing that was immediately clear, however, was that it was in a dreadful condition. Its coat was no more than a mass of filthy, matted hair and its eyes were so infected and filled with puss that it clearly couldn't see. And, not surprisingly, the little mite was totally terrified.

With some difficulty, as the dog was snapping in a pathetic effort to defend itself, the volunteer was able to get the dog into a carrier and to take it to a Veterinary Surgeon, who was forced to heavily sedate the dog before he could begin to examine it.

The first problem to be addressed was the condition of the dog's eyes and there was initially concern that it might be blind; fortunately such fears proved to be groundless. Then the revolting lumps of matted hair were shaved off to reveal a coat of pure white. And just like the Hans Christian Andersen tale, this little ugly duckling turned into a beautiful swan. Or, more accurately, a gorgeous little Bichon Frise.

Once the Vet had completed his work and restored the little girl's physical health, Rene, as she was named, was transferred to the Bianca shelter where the task began of restoring her faith in humans. It was far from an easy undertaking as, not surprisingly, Rene was more than a little wary of people but slowly, day by day, through patience and care, she was won over.

As her confidence grew, so did her coat until she was eventually restored to the beautiful little creature that she had obviously once been, a long time ago. Once they were convinced that she was ready, Bianca was able to find a new home for Rene.

And for Rene, or Peauty as she is now known, the horrors of that beach are now no more than a distant memory as she revels in the love and attention she receives and of which she was clearly deprived for far too long.

# 🐾HOW TO TRAIN🐾
# CHILDREN

Initially I thought of making this a short chapter. Very short indeed. Two words in fact. Namely "impossible" and "pointless".

But then I thought of all my four legged friends who had passed pet shop windows, looking longingly at the rawhide chews and other delicacies on display. And yet had shown great restraint by not pulling their owner inside, but instead saved all their pennies so that one day, one special day, they could afford this very volume. Safe in the knowledge that if they followed the advice this book contained, their lives could be changed for the better. And that is when I decided that I couldn't short change them with a mere two words, irrespective of how appropriate they were.

So I thought, if I can't tell you how to train them, I could at least devote this chapter to explaining a little about these strange little creatures known as children.

It is said that humans constantly seek answers to three great questions:

1. Is there a God?

2. Is there life on other planets?

3. Will there ever be anything even remotely funny on an episode of "Miranda"?

In my view, however, they need to add a fourth question:

4. Why have children?

To be honest, having studied the matter for many years I still haven't come up with a definitive answer to that one. You see when children are young they simply are disgusting (more later), objectionable and very expensive to rear. That would seem bad enough if it wasn't for the fact that just when they seem to be turning into actual human beings that might contribute something to family life, they change into that most odious of all creatures, "the teenager", where meaningful conversation is replaced by a series of grunts and who would cut off a leg with a rusty knife rather than admit they were in any way related to their poor, long suffering parents.

Show me a human who tells you that life with a teenager is pleasant in any shape or form and I'll show you someone who could give little old Pinocchio a run for his money. So, knowing full well that the small bawling, smelly, drooling, obnoxious little creatures, that invariably deprive adult humans of regular sleep for years, will one day turn into teenagers why do they bother having them?

The best theory I can come up with is that humans have an obsession with "sharing". For some reason best known to them they want to "share their life and their love with others"; yup, time to pass the sick bag. Personally I reckon that the whole concept of sharing is deeply flawed. But if they want to give away something just to make themselves feel good, then more fool them.

Right. Having established that, like it or not (and I know which of those options I would go for), the average dog will have to share their home with a least one child. So why can't I advise you on how to go about training them? As I said earlier, training children is both impossible and pointless.

Why impossible you no doubt ask? Simply because children are so slow in learning anything new. Even the dumbest dog on the block was toilet trained by the time it was a few months old. And yet you will find kids three years old wandering around with a bag attached and filled with ....I trust you get the picture without me going into graphic detail and putting us all off our tea. "Oh come on Anna" I hear you say "pull one of the other three". But no, it's true. Three years old and still carrying their ....well you know what I mean...with them. So if they can't even learn how to go to the loo, how can you possibly hope to teach them anything that is beneficial to you?

And if you did end up with one of above average intelligence (and they are few and far between, believe me) who might just be trainable, what would the point be anyway?

Small children appear to have only one ability (assuming you don't count dribbling, throwing up, breaking things and such as "abilities") and that is the talent to cry. Now the average little pup will give the occasional whimper. True. But a whimper is a sweet and gentle sound. A child's cry has a decibel level similar to a 747 as it takes off and all the charm and tone of your average X Factor contestant. And while a puppy will generally only whimper for three reasons – "I'm lonely", "I'm hungry", "I need out" - the list of reasons why a kid wails is truly endless. It can mean "I don't want to go to bed, I don't want THAT food, I want lifted, I want put down, I don't want to sit in my high chair, I don't want to go into my car seat. I don't want to have my nappy changed etc etc". And then when they get that bit older they invent a brand new set of complaints such as "I want to sit in a supermarket trolley, I don't want to sit in a supermarket trolley, I don't want to go to school, I want to play with Tracey, I hate Tracey and I never want to see her again" Ad infinitum. In truth I could go on and on with this for pages but I don't want to waste paper; after all it doesn't grow on trees*.

But what if we could train them when they were little; wouldn't that benefit us when they grew up? Well no, for as I explained earlier they metamorphosis into teenagers and trust me you don't want to have anything to do with them. True by that age they would be able to take you for a walk although I doubt if either of their down trodden parents would be brave enough to suggest it. But ask yourself this question – would you really want to be seen by your friends being dragged around the streets by something that looks like it only learned to walk upright earlier that day, that appears to have acquired its clothes from the discarded bin at the back of a Salvation Army shelter and that has long lank hair, that has never had more than a nodding acquaintance to Vosene shampoo, all topped off with a huge stupid baseball cap worn, if that's the right term in these circumstances, sideways? Not even in the darkest night in the depths of winter when the street lights had failed would I chance being spotted accompanying that.

So let's just move on and accept that as far as training is concerned, children are a lost cause. Mind you I must admit that it is not just teenagers who can become a problem; dogs of a certain age i.e. the terrible twos can be just as difficult. I recently overheard "him" and a friend, who happens to be Baxter the Cockerdoodle's owner, speaking about problems she was encountering. I must admit that I did eavesdrop; come on we all enjoy a bit of gossip.

*"It's really terrible. He was such a lovely wee boy but recently he has started adopting this "whatever" attitude when I'm trying to get him to follow my command. So I throw a ball and he chases after it, I say 'bring it!' and he'll get it and canter back so far but then drop it on the ground half way back to me and nonchalantly wander off to sniff more trees, or ideally, a dog butt. I complain about his attitude and making me walk to collect the damn ball, and his surly reply is usually "hey, you said bring it, you didn't say how far".*

But to return to children and to what may perhaps be a surprising admission - there are minor advantages in sharing a home with them. For a start the average teenager can wind up "him" and "her" in ways that we canines can only dream of. And with so little effort. A simple shrug of the shoulders or a mumbled "so unfair" and your humans will turn a strange colour of purple and start emitting smoke from their ears. Sheer class.

But even more important are children's eating habits. It starts at a very early age with food being thrown from a high chair, which you have no doubt positioned yourself just below.

Okay, I know some of the stuff they are fed is pretty disgusting but remember, I'm a Labrador and everything is edible. And then when they get older, rebellion involves picking at anything put in front of them for no other reason than "she" cooked it. That's the time to cosy up to "her", who is at her most vulnerable, and to look up with the biggest doe eyes you can muster. Before she can finish saying "well somebody appreciates my cooking", you'll find your plate filling up with barely touched home cooked food.

Kids? Yes, I reckon every home should have one.

*Yes I do know. It was a joke.

Dogs should never play poker.

"Guess who's got a good hand?"

Dogs should never miss the chance to wind-up their human

"That's it. Ears up. They'll think you've heard somebody
prowling about outside"

# Tired of all those common cross breeds?

LOOKING FOR A NEW BREED TO IMPRESS YOUR NEIGHBOURS?
WELL LOOK NO FURTHER, JUST VISIT

## THE GREEDYBLEEDERBREEDER STUD

READY SOON **COCKAPOOGOLDENOODLELAB PUPS**

OR WHY NOT BRING ALONG A SKETCH OF HOW YOU WOULD LIKE
YOUR NEW DOG TO LOOK AND LET OUR TEAM OF DESIGNERS
PRODUCE SOMETHING TRULY ORIGINAL – JUST FOR YOU?

DON T WASTE TIME LOOKING AT BORING OLD PEDIGREES
OR VISITING THOSE GHASTLY RESCUE CENTRES
(MOST OF THEIR DOGS THERE ARE JUST MONGRELS ANYWAY).

COME ALONG TO THE GREEDYBLEEDERBREEDER STUD
WHERE D ISN T FOR DOG, IT S FOR DESIGNER
AND GET YOURSELVES A TRULY ORIGINAL CROSS BREED.

EVERY PUP COMES WITH A GUARANTEE TO HAVE A VERY SILLY
BREED NAME AND TO COST FASHIONABLY LARGE SUMS OF CASH

(SECOND MORTGAGES CAN BE ARRANGED)

# Stories from the Shelter

## LADY

Someone appearing at the gates of the Bianca shelter with an unwanted dog is far from an unusual event. Indeed never a week goes past that at least one animal, suddenly surplus to requirements, isn't surrendered for re-homing.

Most people have the good grace to stay and hand over their pet, although finding dogs tied up to the perimeter is a regular occurrence. On one memorable occasion, a man dressed himself up in women's clothing and a wig before dumping an animal at the gate to the shelter. His disguise might have proved effective in concealing his identity if his car, complete with number plate, hadn't been caught on the CCTV camera and the authorities were informed.

It is fair to say that most animals given up are young; a box of pups is very common and Bianca is always happy to take them in. What is much less likely is for someone to give up a dog that they had had for many years. A dog like Lady.

Lady is a Portuguese Pointer, a type of small hunting dog. But Lady's life hadn't been spent hunting. Her life had been devoted to doing nothing more than producing litter after litter of puppies.

But then Lady grew old and her owner clearly saw no point in keeping a 13 year old bitch that couldn't make him any money. So Lady was offered up to Bianca.

But the lack of future litters wasn't the only reason that her owner was particularly anxious to be rid of her. For on the day that Lady arrived at the shelter the volunteers noticed that she had great difficulty in walking as a consequence of a huge untreated hernia, the size of a small football, between her back legs.

Following an examination by Bianca's Vet, a decision had to be made on the old girl's future. Should she undergo more than one operation and at her age would she be fit to do so? The Vet confirmed that other than the unsightly hernia, Lady was in remarkably good health and all agreed that she should be given the chance to enjoy life for however short a time she had left.

Lady in fact required three operations but came through them without any ill effects and when she recovered obviously felt a much healthier and happier little dog without the grotesque lump between her legs. And so, after a brief spell in the shelter, Bianca began to look for a new home for Lady.

It clearly wasn't easy to find a suitable home for a dog of her age and background but the charity struck gold and Lady suddenly found herself flying off to a new life in Sweden. As you can see, she was not only introduced to the fun of playing in the snow, resplendent in a very smart new coat, but much more importantly at last discovered the delights of living in a loving and caring home.

# ❀ TREAT YOUR OWNER TO ❀ A WIND UP

At this point in the book I thought we could all do with a short break from the serious and arduous work of owner training and to partake of a little light relief.

We dogs all have different ways of enjoying ourselves, some of which, I must admit, totally mystify me. I mean why would any dog want to spend its days in a cold, draughty building running round and round interminably, jumping over wooden hurdles, weaving through posts and crawling through tunnels? And all at speeds that suggest that someone has just tied a large lit firework to their tail. All that energy expended for what? One little treat if they are lucky!

Weird if you ask me.

My idea of enjoying myself is to have a large leisurely breakfast, a decent walk with masses of time for regular sniffing and consumption of anything "edible"* I come across, followed by a long doze on a comfy settee.

To my mind there is no comparison between these two pastimes but I guess one dogs' imitation meat is another's poison. But one thing that every single member of the domesticated canine species would undoubtedly agree on is that there is no other pastime that comes even close to

41

providing us with such limitless and unbridled fun and endless amusement as winding up your owner.

I don't intend spending pages and pages detailing a long list of wind ups; half of the fun is inventing and perfecting your own. What I will do, however, is point you in the right direction by telling you about a couple of my own particular favourites.

The first, which I poetically call "the pointless walk", is relatively simple but very effective if employed in the correct manner and in the right circumstances. Before I start, I must issue a few warnings. Firstly, and most importantly, remember and get out to the garden for a long pee during the evening if you intend employing this little exercise; the joke would be on you not your owner if you end up spending a long and uncomfortable night with your back legs tightly crossed. Secondly don't repeat it too often; eventually they'll get wise to what is going on (yes I know they can be a bit slow but ultimately it will dawn on even the dimmest human) and it will fall apart. And thirdly, and most importantly, chose your evening for this wind up very, very carefully.

And the "right evening" for maximum effect is one that is a truly horrible night weather wise. Heavy rain is fine. Snow is even better, especially if accompanied by a wind blowing all the way from the North Pole. Once you are satisfied that you have the "perfect" evening you wait until "they" start preparing to go to bed and then you put on that pathetic look and stand staring longingly at the front door. If that doesn't instantly have the desired effect, the addition of a small whimper should suffice.

And so "he"** takes pity on you and fetches your lead. But if you have chosen wisely, he will also have to go and get his a. Waterproof trousers, b. Heavy jacket, c. Walking boots, d. Gloves and e. Woolie hat. And if this miserable night follows a spell of good weather, you can enjoy the added bonus of watching him scurry around the house looking for all these items, often coupled with him and her having a little "chat" about where he left them and just why she insists on moving everything etc., etc.

Where I live there is an area of trees relatively close to our house – close but far enough away in a blizzard. So once "he" has finally got all these clothes on, I pull him along the road towards the trees and listen contentedly to him muttering to himself about the bleep bleep weather. And then just at the very moment I reach the wooded area I stop dead in my tracks and stare into space. I refuse to move in any direction and decline to "perform". It drives him nuts. Eventually when I am convinced that I have achieved maximum annoyance (usually when he has started to resemble a very grumpy snowman) I turn around, having done nothing in the toilet department, and walk home again, accompanied by even louder mutterings. Magic.

But in my book (and after all this IS my book) nothing beats "the morning wind up". Before I explain it to you I should paint a picture of breakfast time chez Gibb. Following a wander along to the local wood (yup the very same one) for my morning toilet break***, we return to the kitchen where we enjoy a family breakfast in a jolly civilised manner. Well we do until Mr. & Mrs. Slob decide that they need to adjourn to the lounge with a cup of tea in one hand and a syrupy slice of toast in the other so they can continue to watch the muppets**** on BBC's Breakfast show.

Once when I were but a lass, I would foolishly "ask out" (jump about and stare pathetically at the vestibule door etc – I'm sure you all know the drill) as they exited the kitchen en route for the lounge. What a silly girl I was. Where was the fun in that? Eventually, however, it dawned on me that it would cause them much more upset if I waited until they actually sat down before I made my demand.

And gradually over the course of time (this has been going on every morning for years now and remarkably they still haven't twigged as to what is happening) I have modified and honed it until I have got it just right. I now wait until they have both got themselves comfortably settled on the settee, have the T.V. turned on and have just begun the consumption of their tea and toast before I make my request to be let out. The sound of the grumping, as one of them has to get up, find a suitable spot to temporarily deposit the breakfast items including sourcing a coaster or the like to ensure that the furniture doesn't get marked, and move to the door, is pure music to my ears.

And that, of course, is only half the fun. For the coup de grace***** is delivered by barking to get back in provided, and I can't stress this strongly enough, this request is timed just right. And that can be a little tricky. Too soon and they haven't settled back down fully; too long and they may have finished eating and drinking and have headed back to the kitchen.

But assuming that you will want to follow my example and adopt a similar wind up, you will need to know the optimum time between being allowed out and requesting to be let back in. And here for the very first time I can reveal it to you all. It is .....wait for it, wait for it....28.3 seconds, as has been proven by extensive clinical testing******. That gives them just enough time to have picked up said tea and toast, sat back down and started watching the T.V. again.

Timed right it is pretty close to perfection although I can occasionally add a little icing on the cake by getting it to coincide with a T.V. moment they have been waiting for. In his case it can be highlights of a particularly brilliant hat trick by Lionel Messi or some new theatre work being unveiled on Broadway or a dozen other items; in her case, it usually involves George Clooney.

As I said earlier this wasn't meant to be the definitive guide to winding up your human, merely a few pointers to let you devise your own schemes. If you are one of the more energetic dogs i.e. not a Lab, then you might like to follow the example of a Jack Russell friend of mine who, on a forest walk, often pretends to run off after a rabbit or a deer but in truth merely hides behind a tree until the shouts of "Barney" reach a pitch seldom achieved, even by opera singers, and the kids begin to cry, before reappearing to be greeted with hugs and kisses.

So don't delay, start winding up your owner today.

*dogs and humans often have different ideas of what is edible but how can "they" describe certain things we find and consume as "disgusting" if they haven't tried it themselves?

**if it is raining or snowing it will invariably be "he" who is involved

***an excellent little wind up is to perform your morning number twos in stages so that "they" eventually run out of poo bags and have to search through all their pockets for a scrap of paper which, if you are really fortunate, will prove inadequate in dimensions for the purpose with truly hilarious results

****no not those Muppets; it was merely a derisory term for those smarmy morning TV presenters

*****a little bit of French for all my Poodle pals

****** by me, who did you think?

# ☙ TRAIN YOUR OWNER TO ☙ COOK

I should begin this chapter by saying that 50% of the humans that I share a home with can cook. And do I really have to tell you which half of the "him and her" combo that is? Oh I do? Sorry I forget from time to time that all breeds aren't as intelligent as us Labradors. It's "her".

Okay "he" does "cook" a couple of times a week and looks like a dog with two tails* when he presents his masterpiece to her. I don't want to embarrass him (well actually that is a total lie) but his "cooking" can be summed up in seven stages:

1. Go to Marks and Spencer and buy the food (only when the Dine for 2 for £10 deal is on – he's too mean to buy their food at full price).

2. Turn on the oven.

3. Read the instructions on the packets.

4. Place the plastic containers of food on a baking tray and put in the oven.

5. Wait until the prescribed time has elapsed.

6. Remove from the oven and empty the contents of the plastic containers onto two plates.

## 7. Serve

Not a hugely difficult task you would have thought and yet as they tuck in, he invariably sits there with a self-satisfied look on his face, no doubt regarding himself as Saga version of Jamie Oliver.

And, of course, like all male humans he barbeques and has that amazing ability that they all seem to possess of being able to cook a hamburger so that it is charred to a cinder on the outside but still red raw in the middle. Still it is worth hanging around when he is working the old BBQ as he is a pretty messy worker and invariably drops some of the food he is cooking. And on those occasions I act as Daddy's little helper and help clean up the mess.

But enough about "him". This chapter is aimed at educating all our "hers". As I said at the start, she cooks and bakes and judging by the reaction she engenders, seems pretty good at both. Of course she's had lots of practice, having cooked for him for decades, for my human "brother and sister" for almost as long while now she bakes with the older of the "little darlings". Along the way she has also cooked for extended members of the family and friends from near and far, for a pack of cubs at a camp, for the homeless in their temporary accommodation, for huge numbers of the congregation of her church and many, many more people, too numerous to mention.

Now why don't we have a little quiz? And unlike that programme that is on BBC TV every night, the one with the haughty know-it-all with the stupid glasses, this one isn't "pointless". This is a very short quiz, one question only. Ready? "Who is missing from the long list of people "her indoors" has cooked and baked for over the years?" Well done, you got it in one. Yes, the correct answer is, of course, ME.

Okay on a couple of occasions when I've been a bit off colour she has made me a scrambled egg but scrambling an egg isn't proper cooking; I mean even "he" could do that. Actually, come to think of it, he probably couldn't. But you get my jist.

I suspect that most of you have suffered the same fate with your "hers", but now, for the first time, they can no longer hide behind that old chestnut "oh I wouldn't know what to cook/ bake for a dog" for thanks to Aunt Heather and her faithful canine companion Bernie, who selflessly offered to taste all of these recipes for her (several times in fact), we have food for you and me that didn't....wait for it...come out of a packet or a tin. Now isn't that a breakthrough?


*No, I've never seen a dog with two tails either.

# BERNIE'S BEEFIE STEW

## Ingredients
1 cup hamburger meat
2 hard-boiled eggs, chopped
1/2 cup cooked brown rice
2 jars of baby food veggies (peas, green beans, carrots, spinach)
2 tbsp fat-free cottage cheese
1 tbsp olive oil

## Cooking instructions
In a pan, cook meat with olive oil.
Once meat is brown, drain excess grease from meat. Then, add eggs, rice, cottage cheese and vegetables.
Mix well.
Let food cool to room temperature.

## Serving size
Approx. 2 - 3 cups

# BERNIE'S BONEY COOLERS

## Ingredients
2 fresh beef (or other species) marrow bones,
each at least 1 inch long
Water

## Cooking Instructions
In about a 2 qt pan, put the bones,
and add enough water to cover the bones.
Bring water to a boil;
continue to boil for at least 10 min.
(More time is ok for a richer broth.)
Remove bones, and return any beef
marrow to the liquid along with any meat
that you can get off the bones.
Cool the broth to room temperature.
Pour liquid only into 2-4 ice cube trays.
Chop up the marrow/meat/gristle into
little bits, and put them into each
section of the tray. Freeze solid.

Serve 2-3 cubes on a very hot day.
(Not too many if you made the broth
very rich with extra bones or lots
of marrow.)

# BERNIE'S BIANCA BISCUITS

## Ingredients

1/2 cup water
1/2 cup oil
2 eggs
3 tablespoons peanut butter
(natural if possible)
2 1/2 cups whole wheat flour
1/2 cups oats

## Baking Instructions

Add wet ingredients to dry and mix well.
Transfer to a floured surface and knead
until dough holds together.
Roll out until about 1/2 inch thick
and cut with cookie cutters.
Bake on a parchment lined
cookie sheet for 30 minutes at 375°f.
Cool on a wire rack.

# BERNIE'S BREAKFAST BARS

## Ingredients

12 c. oatmeal
4 c. whole wheat flour
8 eggs
¾ c. oil
2/3 c. honey
½ c. molasses
2 c. milk
1 large can solid pack pumpkin
(optional, not pie filling)
3 to 4 mashed bananas (optional)

## Cooking Instructions

Preheat oven to 325°f. Grease 2 cookie sheets.
Dump everything into a VERY large bowl.
Mix this whole mess together, pat onto
greased cookie sheets & bake at 325°f
for 1 hour.   After 1 hour turn oven off,
open oven door
&
allow cookies to cool in the oven.
Break into whatever size you want.

These also freeze very well.

# BERNIE'S POOCHIE CAKES

## Ingredients

1 ½ cups brown rice / 3 cups water
2 large potatoes, grated /
4 large carrots, grated
2 large celery stalks, chopped
6 pounds ground beef
8 eggs
1 dash salt / ¼ cup olive oil
1 ½ cups regular rolled oats

## Cooking Instructions
1. Preheat oven to 400 °F
(205 degrees C).
Grease 36 cups of 3 large muffin tins.
2. In a medium saucepan,
combine the rice with water.
Bring to a boil over high heat,
uncovered, and cook 10 minutes.
Reduce heat to low, cover,
and simmer 20 minutes.
Remove from heat, let cool several
minutes, then fluff with a fork
and set aside.

BERNIE'S POOCHIE CAKES *continued*

3. In a large bowl, combine the potatoes, carrots, celery, ground beef, and eggs. Mix ingredients together using your hands or a sturdy spoon. Add salt, olive oil, rolled oats, and rice; mix well.

4. Fill each muffin cup with some of the meat mixture, and pat down the mixture to make it firm. Bake 45 minutes, or until surface feels set. Cool on a rack 10 minutes or longer.

5. Remove the meat cakes by turning the muffin tin upside down over a sheet of aluminum foil. Tap each muffin cup to release the cake. Refrigerate or freeze in sealed plastic bags.

DO NOT FEED TO DOGS WHEN STILL HOT

# DISCLAIMER

All connected with this book accept no responsibility, culpability, answerability, accountability, blame or whatever, if any person, dog, cat, guinea pig, rabbit, or other animal of any description (alive or otherwise) suffers sickness, constipation, diarrhoea, beri beri, malaria, yellow fever, leprosy or any other disease known to human kind or not yet discovered as a result of following these recipes.

Cooking and baking using these recipes is carried out 100% (110% in the case of footballers) at your owner's own risk and Aunt Heather, her relatives, her neighbours, her friends, that nice couple she met on holiday in Edinburgh last year and anyone else who has ever known her, accept no liability of any description.

So please don't bother getting Shyster & Son, Solicitors, to call her.

# Stories from the Shelter

# KING

The volunteers at the Bianca shelter are all too used to animals arriving with broken legs. Indeed barely a week goes past without at least one unfortunate creature suffering from such an injury being left in Bianca's care.

And as the economic situation in Portugal has worsened, sadly so has this problem with an increasing number of pet owners simply abandoning their animals who, devoid of road sense, invariably end up the unfortunate victims of vehicles.

But despite having dealt with all too many cases of animals injured in this manner, it is fair to say that no one at the shelter was quite prepared for King.

Ana from the shelter was on a mission to try and get a local man to spay his bitch when she first became acquainted with King, a Jack Russell type puppy. The pup was clearly in a distressed state and it transpired that it had been knocked down by a car, as a consequence of which one of its front legs was both broken and very severely gashed. Ana established that the accident had occurred eight days earlier and yet the pup's owner did not seek any Veterinary help but merely wrapped the leg in an old piece of gauze, allowing the poor mite to suffer unimaginable pain for eight long days and nights.

Ana was asked to take the little dog with her, which she was more than happy to do, and brought it to the Bianca shelter where, very gently, the piece of filthy gauze was removed from the dog's leg. The disgusting smell that emanated from the injured limb instantly alerted the Bianca volunteers to the fact that gangrene had already set in.

Although King was instantly rushed to a Vet, everyone at the shelter knew that it was already too late to save the poor lad's leg and all that could be done was to remove the leg and save the dog's life.

As he recovered in the surgery, it became clear that King held no grudges. Indeed he faithfully followed the staff around and was always ready for a cuddle. And in a remarkably short space of time King was fit and ready to return to the shelter.

Of all the traits that are possessed by dogs, but sadly not by humans, the ability not to feel sorry for themselves is high up the list. All that the pup had gone through in his short life was instantly forgotten as he was introduced to all the other pups and young dogs at the shelter and joined in their games of chasing each other around and having mock battles.

Being balanced on a tripod, King was at somewhat of a disadvantage and he was invariably bowled over and ended up on his back. But as the old song says, he just picked himself up, dusted himself down and started all over again.

His life had undoubtedly taken a dramatic upward turn and yet even better times lay ahead, as not one but two guardian angels lay in store.

In March 2013, Anne and Tine decided to follow the example of friends in Belgium and to go and volunteer at the Bianca shelter, arriving with suitcases filled to bursting with donations of medicines and the like supplied by various veterinaries and animal companies they had approached in Belgium and the U.K.

In Tine's own words "The first time you enter the shelter, it is overwhelming. All the beasties are barking at the new people arriving, their little tails are all going crazy, the tiny faces are all looking at you, asking for attention... Yes, I really think "overwhelming" is the most appropriate word to use"

Anne and Tine quickly discovered that life in the shelter is constantly busy and there are always jobs to do and chores to be carried out as well as the highly important task of "socialising" the dogs and puppies, an essential part of getting abused and abandoned animals ready for adoption.

Several times a day the many puppies at the shelter get out of their enclosures to let off steam, and to allow the shelter staff to clean out the kennels, and Tine and Anne always knew when the puppies were going to be let out and always made sure they were there to watch the madness!

And as the girls sat on the ground with all the puppies around them, they were introduced for the very first time to little King. Although all the animals made an indelible mark on them both, the girls soon ended up with a long list of favourites. And top of Tine's list was undoubtedly King.

On returning to Belgium, Tine gave serious thought to adopting the wee fellow and spoke to a long-time family veterinary to ask about keeping a 3-legged dog. Basically she was told that apart from being very careful with exercise and not "over-doing it" (they knew the dog had certain limitations - but he didn't), it would be no different from having a 4-legged dog.

Several weeks later Anne and Tine were waiting impatiently at Schipol Airport in Amsterdam for the arrival of eight dogs from the Bianca shelter, including a certain little three legged rascal.

Within days the wee lad was relishing his new life (and garden!) and had become a bit of local celebrity. The dark days of his accident and all the pain and suffering that ensued, long forgotten by The King of Portugal.

# 🐾 TRAIN YOUR OWNER TO 🐾 DRESS

You may wonder why we dogs need to concern ourselves with how our owners dress. Well wonder no more for I am about to enlighten you. There are two main reasons, the first of which can be best described as "dressing practically".

In truth there is never a problem with "him" dressing practically. Embarrassingly yes – but we'll get to that later.

No the problem is with "her". Unlike him her outfit changes from day to day in a desperate but ultimately futile effort to get all her clothes worn. So "what is the problem?" you are no doubt wondering. Before I divulge it, let us all partake of a little light relief in the form of a "joke", a form of jocular entertainment much beloved by humans.

A human goes into a pet shop and asks the owner

"Do you have any unusual pets?".

The pet shop owner thinks for a moment, goes through to the back shop and returns with a centipede which he informs the shopper, can talk.

The centipede promptly displays this talent by chatting politely about the weather and the like.

Clearly delighted, the shopper buys the centipede and all the way home in the car, the little creature talks and talks. They have dinner together during which time the centipede, while not nibbling on a lettuce leaf, proves to be an interesting conversationalist.

While he is the kitchen washing up the dishes the man decides that he should take the centipede down to his local pub so he can show him off to all his mates. So he shouts through to the centipede

"Why don't you and I nip down to my local?".

Silence.

He tries again but there is still not a sound from the little creature.

Eventually, getting annoyed, the human bellows "I said, why don't we…."

At this point he is interrupted by the centipede.

"I heard you, I heard you. Give me a minute. I'm just putting my shoes on".

Now I am not suggesting that "her indoors" has sufficient shoes in her closet to shod a centipede, but let's just say that the creature wouldn't be left with many cold feet. So why do female humans need so many pairs of shoes, when after all they only have two feet? Sorry, I may be a bit of genius but that little mystery is frankly beyond me.

Certainly I'll admit that her shoe closet boasts a very wide variety of species of footwear. There are….well let me put it this way

*Black shoes, brown shoes, long shoes that look like clown shoes,*

*Shoes of blue and cream and grey, and every shade of tan,*

*Croc skin, snake skin, too tight shoes that break skin,*

*She now owns every type of shoe that is known to man.*

Thought I would liven things up with a bit of poetry\*. In truth the final line should have read *In fact she owns every type of shoe that is known to man with one exception* but that wouldn't have rhymed so it had to be abandoned. And we will come to that one exception in a minute, once I have highlighted another strange enigma that surrounds female humans and their foot fetishes. For the world of shoe sales is governed by the law of diminishing returns.

For a relatively small sum in human money, you can buy a pair of substantial shoes with lots of leather, big thick soles, long hard wearing laces and more. Multiply that price by ten and what do you get? A thin little sole, criss -crossed with two pencil thin pieces of leather, balanced on a silly spike heel so high that it makes the wearer look like they are training to walk on stilts. And, of course, most importantly of all, a name stamped on the sole. No, not the wearer's name dummy. A "designer" name. It doesn't matter how well made shoes are, what they are made of and even what they look like as long as they can boast a designer tag.

*Givenchy shoes, Gucci shoes, shoes you can say are Jimmy Choos,*

*Shoes made to measure and shoes bought "off the peg",*

*Zara shoes, Chloe shoes, ugly but showy shoes,*

*Shoes that fit your feet but cost an arm and a leg\*\**

I am not suggesting that "her indoors" buys designer shoes – I'd love to see "his" face if she came home with a pair of those with the price still on the box – but she certainly has a varied selection of footwear. With, as I hinted, earlier, one exception. "Sensible" shoes. As far as sensible shoes are concerned, her motto seems to be "Not in my closet". And it is for that very reason that I was forced to embark on a campaign of training her to dress.

If you are still confused with where the problem lies, try to imagine going out with your human after a night of heavy rain. You would assume that your human would be astute enough to be prepared to come across puddles. Sadly my "her", until I showed her the error of her ways, didn't want to consider such a possibility and would wear a pair of shoes not because they were suitable to encounter a wet path but because they matched whatever jacket she had chosen to wear that particular day.

And, of course, within two minutes of setting off we encountered our first watery obstacle which she endeavoured, and failed, to tip toe over. By the time we had reached puddle number three, her feet were well and truly wet, my lead was on and we were headed back home. My walk curtailed through nothing more than her failure to dress sensibly.

After this happened several times, I realised that immediate training was essential and I set about rectifying the situation. The solution was remarkably simple, albeit not without an element of risk, and involved me heading off through the wettest, marshiest area of grass I could find the instant I was let out of the car. I also adopted the common canine medical condition known as "selective deafness". After I had failed to "hear" several calls requesting my immediate return, she was eventually forced to plod after me. When we returned home her feet weren't so much wet as truly saturated and caked with mud and she was practically in tears because her "best pair of medium grey loafers" *** were totally ruined.

The reason I added a codicil about risk above is that if you are stuck with a female human who values her shoes above her faithful companion (and many would, believe me) then you could end up spending long hours just staring out the window at other dogs enjoying their constitutional. Fortunately my "her" is a sweet old thing and she went and invested in a pair of sturdy walking boots**** (which she changes into before we walk – you didn't think she would wear them leaving the house did you?) and all in the garden, and the muddy forest walk, was rosy.

So having disposed of the practical, let's turn our attention to the second reason for training your human to dress properly. Namely, to allow you to avoid embarrassment.

I am sure many of us have encountered this scenario. You are out for a forest walk when you spot another dog coming along the path towards you, accompanied by a human who looks like he or she has just stepped straight out of "Country Life", or one of those other glossy magazines so beloved by the "set" whose idea of a pleasant pastime is to murder innocent and unsuspecting creatures. You glance over your shoulder to check how your "he" is dressed and instantly start looking for a tree large enough to hide behind.

As I alluded to earlier "he" always dresses practically. He has two outfits, one for winter and the other for pretty much the rest of the year. The winter version comprises of a Regatta jacket in a colour that could best be described as "faded bilious green" which he bought from a gentleman's outfitters in rural Perthshire that was established, and last brought in new stock, just before the Boer war. The ensemble is completed by a pair of black cords (M & S end of season sale) which have become rubbed at the knees. Now I know that denim jeans with tears at the knees were once fashionable (you really could sell humans ANYTHING, couldn't you?) but cords with rubbed knees. I don't think so.

Outfit two comprises of a fleece of unknown make in a colour that could be best described as "very faded bilious green" and a pair of black cords with rubbed knees. Yes the same ones. Both outfits are completed with a pair of boots or shoes, sensible naturally, chosen from his somewhat meagre shoe closet. Never mind a centipede, he would have difficulty accommodating the footwear needs of a spider.

But while my "he" dresses embarrassingly, at least I am not stuck with "Designer Man". You must have come across him. Every single item of clothing he wears has a "badge" on it just to make sure you realise how expensive it was. And in the off chance that he meets someone who is a bit short sighted, he displays a horse on his Polo shirt roughly the same size as Shergar (before he was made into dog food that is).

But if you think that is bad, spare a thought for all those poor canines that have to go out accompanied by "Cheapskate Designer Man". He is the one that wants to wear nothing but Calvin Klein, Paul Smith, Ralph Lauren and the like but is too mean to pay the inflated prices the shops charge. So he waits not only for the shops to have a sale, but for that sale to reach the final hour on the final day to buy, undaunted by the fact that everything with any class and style has long gone and that the only sizes left can best be described as "Emaciated Model" and "Eric Pickles".

When he sees the shop assistants giggling behind their hands and preparing for the party the manager promised them if they "ever sold THAT jacket" you would think he might twig. But he is so deliriously happy that he is now the proud owner of a genuine Lacoste jacket (i.e. one that didn't originate in Thailand) that he is totally oblivious to the fact that it is puce with purple stripes or that it is several sizes too small or too large for him.

How will you recognise this sad creature? Not difficult to be honest. If you see someone coming towards you wearing a light coloured raincoat which is open, despite the fact that it is lashing of rain, so that everyone can spot the Burberry lining you've found one. A coat that is so large that he looks like he is trying to find a suitable piece of grass so he can pitch it and live in it. Or if you see someone having difficulty walking in a pair of yellow trousers, so bright they can actually be seen from space, that look like they have been painted on, you know you've found another.

So how can all of us avoid the embarrassment caused by our male human's total lack of dress sense? Well, much as I hate to admit it, I'm bemused. For if they are related to old Ebenezer or alternatively are a poser there is sadly not much you and I can do about it.

Best I can come up? Always chose a walk where there are large trees.

*this little ditty will prove even more edifying to those from the North East of Scotland who are familiar with the tune of the Harry Gordon song (made famous by Scotland The What) "Fittie Folk" to which these jolly witty lyrics (© A. Gibb 2013) can be sung.

**I can only assume this is some strange European currency.

***not be confused with her light grey loafers, her dark grey loafers or her very dark grey nearly black loafers

****must have broken her heart to spend all that money on footwear somewhat devoid of style, the type which is much beloved by bearded men with incredibly boring voices who host TV programmes on the countryside.

# Stories from the Shelter
## LITOS

All dog owners know that fleas can be nuisance and difficult to get rid of once your dog has got them. And yet with all the simple remedies available over the counter at your local pet shop, it is a problem that can be overcome relatively simply and certainly without resorting to drastic measures.

As sadly one Portuguese dog owner did.

Back in 2012 one of the volunteers from the Bianca shelter was driving along a road near Sesimbra in Portugal when she noticed a dog scavenging for food by the side of the road. She stopped the car and approached what appeared to be an elderly and infirm dog and one that seemed to be completely devoid of any hair.

Although the dog, subsequently named Litos, was a little timid she was able to coax it into her car. And only then did she realise that the dog, although clearly undernourished, had bright young eyes and moved in a manner that belied any suggestion that he was elderly.

At that stage, however, the volunteer was unable to reconcile the hairless body with the type of dog concerned but that little mystery was quickly solved by a visit to Bianca's Vet.

An examination by the Vet revealed that Litos wasn't naturally bald. He was totally lacking any hair because it had all been burned off as a consequence of someone covering his body with lime. Although it could never be proven, the Vet was convinced that the lime had been applied by his owner as a cheap method of killing fleas.

It was no doubt effective in that, but in the process it caused the poor little dog indescribable pain and suffering. Treatment of the burns was a long and difficult process but eventually the hair began to grow again turning the pathetic little grey creature into a handsome lad with a deep golden coat.

The problems of malnutrition were also slowly overcome by the people at the shelter and Litos began to look and behave like the young dog that he undoubtedly was. Unfortunately Litos has been diagnosed with leishmaniasis for which he continues to receive regular treatment.

Litos is still looking for a new permanent home but he is a happy lad who enjoys life with his other canine pals at the shelter and revels in the attention, care and love he receives on a daily basis from all at Bianca.

Man's best friend, BUT . . . They don't get sarcasm

Man's best friend, BUT . . . They invented a game they think you enjoy !

# ❧ TRAIN YOUR OWNER TO ❧ WALK

"To move along on foot; to advance by steps; to go on at a moderate pace"     Webster's Dictionary

Humans can walk. Fact. True it does take them a long, long time to master a relatively simply task* but they are able to walk. So why do I need to devote a chapter of this training manual to walking? Because, as old Mister Webster said, walking involves "advancing by steps" and sadly that is where my owners ("him" in particular) fall down. And I know from bitter experience that I am far from alone in suffering from such an affliction.

Before I can explain the problem, I first need to describe the start of the average day in the Gibb household. "Him and her" get up. Eventually. Unless of course the "little darlings" are expected when they are up at the crack of dawn. Other days they aren't so bright eyed and bushy tailed and I have to lie on my lumpy bean bag until they make an appearance.

It wouldn't be so bad if they got up and immediately took me out. But, oh no. First of course they head for the bathroom. Never mind that I haven't been out since the night before while the two of them have just about worn out the lobby carpet tramping back and forth to the loo all night long. To be fair on him, he isn't too bad once he does get up. At least he dresses quickly and gets me out so I can attend to my toilet needs.

But on the odd occasion when it's "her" (if for example, "he" is seriously ill**) it's a total nightmare. Up to the loo. Into the shower. Back to the bedroom. Decides what to wear. Dresses. Decides that something doesn't go with something else. Undresses. Chooses something else. Dresses again. And then, and only then, takes me out. And all this time, I am lying there trying to think of something to take my mind off my predicament and endeavouring to banish thoughts of a patch of fresh cut green grass.

Anyway, lets assume that "he" is up and about and taking me along the road to the wooded area for my morning constitutional. Providing he doesn't meet anyone along the way it normally goes smoothly. Walk along. Poo. Bag deposited in bin. Pee. Walk back home for breakfast. Perfect.

However, things can go rapidly down hill if he bumps into a certain other dog's human. For the purposes of this book let's call this other canine Rosie***, a sweet and quiet little dog with whom I am always happy to pass the time, and who has an owner who seems really nice as humans go and always speaks to me.

So what's the problem you are no doubt wondering? The problem is when my human and Rosie's human meet up and begin to speak. Ten minutes is a quick conversation for those two. Doesn't seem long? Perhaps not, unless they meet at our gate as we go out and I haven't yet had the opportunity of "performing"**** or they meet on the way back and my breakfast is waiting. And on occasions when they both get fully into their verbal stride it can be longer. Much longer.

So what weighty subjects do these great minds debate at such length? The state of the economy? Nope. The situation in North Korea. Not even close. What they talk about is the weather. Well not actually talk about it. Moan about it, in truth. And the worse the weather is, the more they enjoy themselves. In fact when it is a nice day they seem positively gloomy that they have nothing to complain about. Except it being "too hot", of course.

I have never quite understood why humans talk so much about the weather. I mean assuming your name isn't Donald Trump (and let's face it, if it was, you would have changed it long ago) then you probably don't have a private jet at your disposal which would allow you to escape to some warmer climes and therefore can't do anything about it. Yet they drone on and on about how bad it is.

But our neighbourhood doom merchants aren't merely content to complain about the fact that today is rainy/ snowy/ windy/ all three at once (delete as appropriate) but also go on and on about the forecast for the days ahead. And, and here is the real killer, moan about the weather yesterday. And last week. Why? It's past, forget about it, move on.

And then, of course, they indulge in their favourite pastime of all, trying to outdo each other about how much they have suffered as a consequence of the weather.

"That was some rain a week past Sunday, wasn't it?"

"Unbelievable"

"Were you caught in the very heavy rain?"

"Caught in it? I was out when it was really torrential"

"I was soaked through".

"Soaked? I had to come home and change everything I was wearing"

"Change? I had to throw away all my clothes. They would never have dried"

"I got a terrible cold because of it"

"A cold? I got double pneumonia and ended up in the Infirmary on a life support machine"

And so on.

It wouldn't be so bad if that was it for the day but oh no. Go for our morning forest walk and he's off again, sharing pearls of wisdom about the prevailing meteorological conditions with practically everyone he meets (and who doesn't see him coming and is able to take a different path). Sometimes it's just a brief "cold today" in passing but if he bumps into one of the regulars such as Kate and Holly or Judy and Megan's owners, we are off again at full tilt.

And as a consequence, a walk ceases to be "To move along on foot; to advance by steps; to go on at a moderate pace" and instead becomes a case of "advancing a few steps followed by a lot of standing or sitting and waiting patiently".

And here is where I can provide invaluable assistance to anyone who suffers similarly as there is a couple of simple ways that you can get him moving again especially when you are off the lead. One of my favourites is to wander off into the woods, then, making sure that he is watching (I usually wait until he stops to draw breath), I roll about on my back. He instantly assumes I have found something interesting and undoubtedly pungent to roll in. If I can find something highly whiffy, like moist horse poo, so much the better but it doesn't really matter as he will have already concluded that that is exactly what it is and will come roaring towards you like a demented banshee.

If that doesn't work, then what I normally like to do is wait until his back is turned and slowly drift off along the path until I am out of sight. Now humans always seem almost pathologically terrified of losing their dogs and you can guarantee that the moment he realises you are gone he will come rushing along the path yelling your name. This not only gets him moving but has the added advantage of allowing his fellow conversationalist (i.e. listener) the opportunity to make their escape.

Everyone's a winner. Well all except "him" who by this stage is hurrying about frantically convinced he will never see his beloved pet again. But don't feel sorry for him. It may be a tough lesson but it's the only way he'll ever learn.

While you may want to train your human to walk, don't under any circumstances encourage them to run. Why? Well, for a start you don't want your human to look like a runner. Stroll down any country lane and you will find human walkers and their canine companions pleasantly passing the time of the day, looking peaceful and "at one with nature" as they poetically like to say. Runners? They are "focused" which is really a single word that encompasses a bloated red face, a sweat stained vest and eyes popping out of their head like some distressed cartoon character.

But for a selfish, and consequently far more important reason, you don't want them to indulge in this pastime for if they do they invariably leave you behind as they pad miserably along the streets. Or worse still, insist on taking you with them. On a lead! This means that you have to move at their pace and are consequently deprived of the opportunity to stray from the path, to sniff out interesting smells, to shoot the breeze with other dogs. In truth, most of the pleasure of going for a walk. And that doesn't even confront the distressing problem of having a wee or performing other bodily functions while being trailed along at speed.

In case your human has just embarked on a fitness craze that involves jogging, can I offer some words of comfort by explaining the four stages of such a campaign?

*Stage1* This involves joining a jogging group. For some strange reason humans seem incapable of doing any such activity on their own and have to be part of a pack where everyone speaks incessantly and at the same time.

*Stage 2* This focuses on getting the right gear starting off with a pair of state of the art running shoes. These must be bought from a specialist sports shop and differ from the "trainers" they can buy from Matallan or the like in three very important ways. Firstly, they have to have a small tick or three stripes on the side. Secondly, they must come with a 48 page manual that explains in great detail, using words that the average human cannot understand but is highly impressed by, how the shoes are made and the aero dynamics of them and how they breathe blah blah blah. And thirdly, they must cost at least four times that of their less illustrious counterparts. And that is very important when they are in a running group and don't want all the other members sniggering at their "cheap trainers".

The rest of the outfit comprises of a running vest emblazoned with the logo of some forthcoming 10K race (yes I know its ten kilometres but it's really not cool unless you call it "10K") that they have entered for and a pair of running shorts or....no you're not ready to face that particular horror quite yet; I'll come back to it.

*Stage 3* This encompasses meeting the other members of the "gang" and pounding the path with the experienced runners moving some distance ahead least anyone thinks that they associate with the duffers. That stage normally lasts from between three and seven days.

*Stage 4* This involves placing the Nike running shoes, the vest and the shorts into a large plastic sack marked "Save The

Children" or "Cancer Research" and placing it outside the front door so it can be collected and taken to a charity shop.

So don't worry if your owner takes up running; believe me the craze won't last and before you know it you'll be back accompanying them as they once again walk like "normal" humans.

Safe in that knowledge, I think you are now strong enough for me to broach the very delicate subject of the alternative to traditional shorts; skin tight Lycra. I don't know who invented Lycra – if you had invented the second worst***** item of human fashion dress in history then you would want to keep a very low profile too – but obviously it was an experiment that went horribly wrong. Perhaps the makers tested it on some tribe in the darkest Amazonian rain forest who had never heard of mirrors. But for some unknown reason it caught on.

Surely they should have made it illegal for anyone devoid of a svelte physique to wear it. Sadly they didn't and Lycra seems to be especially popular amongst a section of the human population that clearly have a season ticket at McDonalds. And it is that very reason that some poor dogs, already deprived of 99% of the pleasure of their walk, find themselves dispossessed of that remaining 1%. For if it is bad enough being trailed on a lead around an interesting forest path, just try and imagine what it must be like doing it when your only view resembles two very large black jellies during an earthquake.

*I already covered, at length, in "Ask Anna" the fact that a puppy is up and toddling about in 3 weeks while it takes a child a year at least to get off its knees. Pathetic isn't it?

**otherwise known as a cold.

***I've called her that because that's her name.

****No, it's nothing to do with the theatre. I'm just trying to be subtle.

*****Lycra is prevented from sinking to the bottom (sorry) of the chart of human dress horrors by the Fair Isle tank top.

# BERTIE BASSETT HOUND'S
## LABRADOR ALLSORTS

All the flavours
so loved by Labradors
including

### Tangy Twist

Made from the finest sun ripened dog poo, hardened and shaped.

### Stale Sandwich

Layers of rank, mouldy bread, carefully styled into an unforgettable treat.

### Bunny Surprise

Hand picked rabbit droppings carefully arranged around a brulee of soft horse dung.

And much more, designed to appeal to the less discerning palate.

Comes in an edible (cardboard) box

e190g

84

# Stories from the Shelter
# ALIVE & VIVA

The arrival of puppies at the shelter is a very regular occurrence. Indeed in a memorable and hectic spell in the summer of 2012 more than 30 pups arrived in a single month. While it is sad to find a box of pups dumped at the shelter gate Bianca is always eternally grateful that the little things are not subjected to a much worse fate.

For on more than one occasion a volunteer from the shelter has stumbled across pups abandoned in a forest, left there for the foxes to eat.

The people at Bianca obviously have a wealth of "puppy" stories but the events of November, 2012 were, even by their standards, unusual. It all began one night when Ana, the chairperson of Bianca, was visiting someone to discuss work that was required at the shelter. As they stood speaking they became aware of a strange sound, a high pitched wailing. Ana initially thought that it was a consequence of two cats fighting, possibly with one being left in an injured or distressed condition, and went to investigate.

What she found instead, in a rain puddle beside a side road, was a very young, very upset and, fortunately for its own survival, very noisy little pup. She picked up the little dog and tried to comfort it as she carried it to her car. But then on her way back she noticed a plastic bag with something small and black in it and discovered another day old pup.

Sadly this second one wasn't so lucky. He hadn't been found in time. And so the vociferous little survivor became known as Alive.

Alive was taken home by Ana who, with the help of her daughter, began the arduous and harrowing job of caring for a day old pup, the many tasks including two hourly feeds from a baby's bottle. Two hourly, day and night. After a couple of days and once it became clear that the little toot was liable to survive his ordeal, Ana began to consider long term plans for him.

And that is where fate showed its hand. In discussing Alive's plight with Hugo, the Vet that the charity regularly uses, it transpired that his Portuguese Water Dog had just had pups and that they were roughly the same age as the little rescued mite. He suggested that they try and see if their bitch would allow another hungry little mouth to feed, one that she hadn't given birth to herself. And so Hugo and his wife Paula introduced Alive to the nursing Mum who displayed lovely maternal instincts by accepting Alive as one of her own.

Clearly Ana and her daughter could catch up on their sleep and wouldn't have to head for work "dog tired" every day. Well that was the theory, but in practice it didn't quite work out that way. For less than a week later Viva arrived.

Late one night a woman was putting a rubbish bag into a street bin when she noticed something moving on the ground nearby. Closer inspection revealed that the "something" was in fact a tiny pup, its eyes tightly closed and clearly only a couple of days old. The lady wrapped the little girl in a warm blanket and took her to the shelter.

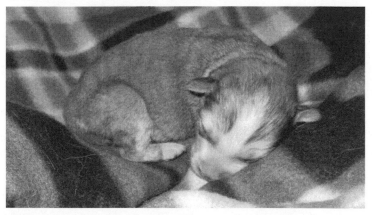

And so Ana and her daughter once again found themselves sharing their house with a little, but rather demanding, creature. They simply couldn't inflict another pup on the poor surrogate mother and so Viva, as she was named, became a guest in Ana's home as the ladies of the house got used, once again, to sleepless nights.

Fortunately both puppies thrived and before too long they were able to join the other wee ones causing havoc in the shelter as homes were sought for them.

A substantial number of the hundreds of dogs that Bianca re-home each and every year go to homes around Europe and it was decided that Alive and Viva would spend their lives in Germany. And so the two little ones, who had begun their lives discarded by the road side, found themselves in Lisbon Airport all set to board an airplane bound for Frankfurt, taking them to carefully selected new homes.

And so the volunteers at Bianca could reflect on a job well done. But yet, within weeks of Alive and Viva's departure, three new born pups were discovered in a rubbish bin, two fortunately still alive, and it began, all over again.

# 🐾 TRAIN YOUR OWNER TO 🐾 BEG

Of all the demeaning things that humans get us to do for their amusement and to show the rest of the world how clever they are, surely begging is pretty high up the list. Personally I have never given "him" or "her" the satisfaction of seeing me sitting there, like one of those hideous china ornaments of dogs they insist on buying, salivating for a tasteless biscuit. Sadly some of my poor brothers and sisters aren't as strong willed and have succumbed to the bribery.

If they want us to have a biscuit then why don't they just give it to us? Quite simply because that wouldn't let our humans show off to everyone else just how clever they are. Now I do use the word "clever" in the very loosest sense, bearing in mind that all they manage to get us to do is sit on our butts with our front paws hanging in the air. Not only an unnatural pose for a four legged creature but a really uncomfortable one as well. Not that our heroic "trainer" cares a jot about how we are suffering.

But even then he or she (look we all know that it is the male humans who behave like this, so let's forget all this him or her nonsense) isn't content with their brilliance. Oh no, he tops it off, not by giving us the treat, but by balancing the biscuit on the end of our nose. Laugh! I thought the carpet would never dry.

And having got us into that totally ridiculous position he then decides that he has to share this display of his brilliance with everyone else in the house. So people are summoned from every corner of the home. Not a problem you would think unless you have Great Aunt Mabel snoring in the lounge. She not only has to be wakened from her slumbers, a far from simple task, but she then has to negotiate the route from lounge to kitchen which she does in a time only slightly faster than Paula Radcliffe takes to complete the London marathon.

And then, at last, when all have told "him" how clever he is and they have all had a jolly good laugh at your expense, you are you allowed to eat the biscuit and are able to return to all fours.

At this point in time you are no doubt expecting me to teach you how to force him to adopt that ridiculous and demeaning position while you go and balance a digestive biscuit on the end of his nose. Thought so. And yes I do appreciate that the front cover hints at that, but that is just artistic license*. Sorry, but it is just not that simple. But don't despair, in certain circumstances it can be achieved, although you will need to enlist "her" help and you will need to live with a family where:

1. "He" is obsessional about something that it is of no practical value whatsoever, and

2. When you need to go to the Vet "he" is the one who takes you.

Before you start jumping up and down with joy, check the wording carefully. All male humans are obsessional about something – reckon it is to do with the fact that although they look like men they are forever little boys in a large, often very large, body. But if that passion is of any practical value to anyone (gardening, DIY etc) then you are in trouble. Fortunately that is a very small percentage of the male population so let's assume you are co-habiting with one of the vast majority and we can start laying plans.

And for those of you with a pessimistic disposition i.e. Bassett Hounds (have you ever seen one that didn't look like it had the troubles of the world on its shoulders?) and worry that they are lumbered with a male human that is not obsessional about something all I can say is – don't. That is about as likely as bumping into a member of the Jimmy Saville Fan Club.

In passing, can I just say if you are lumbered with someone who regards an exciting day out as a visit to Dobie's or B & Q or, on the other hand, a male who refuses to do the Vet run then I'm afraid there is nothing I can suggest. Other than to keep practicing balancing a biscuit on your nose.

Non-practical male addictions can take many forms – following their local football team (or if he is a "glory hunter", a team from hundreds of miles away that he seldom ever gets to see but that is pretty well guaranteed to win trophies), golfing with the boys, fishing trips and loads more. I can't possibly cover every possible scenario so for the purpose of this training exercise let's go with football.

Now this doesn't work any old Saturday as he troops off to the local stadium to mump and moan and arrives home in a foul mood and vows never to go back. You have to wait for a "big game", for example an appearance in a cup final played in the national stadium a long way away*.

So how will you know that such a game is in the offing? Believe me, you'll know. For several weeks prior to the match he will speak of nothing else, morning, noon and night. Then on the week leading up to it, the telephone will never stop ringing, the calls coming from one or other of the "lads" and the lengthy conversations largely centring on whether they think that Sparky*** will have recovered from his groin strain in time.

The rather tatty supporter's scarf will get its annual wash and iron and he will start to lay out the clothes he will wear on the big day which has to include his lucky socks. "Lucky" because he wore them to every previous round of the cup (ignoring the fact that he also wore them the previous year when they got knocked out of the cup in the first round by a team third from the bottom of the lowest league); clearly his beloved team would have no chance of lifting the trophy if he made a mistake and wore a clean pair of socks by mistake.

The day of the game will dawn early and you will be wakened from your slumber at about 5.30 a.m. Yes, that would be a rather silly time to play a football match. In fact it doesn't kick off until 3 p.m. but they have to be up and away with the lark if they are to fit in sufficient pub stops along the way. And that is the last of him you will see that day.

Whatever happens on the hallowed turf he will be back late, and truthfully you don't want to be there to witness his return. If his team has got beat, he will be in a dreadful humour and if they have won....well let's just say he won't be a pretty sight. And while she may have to listen to a kick by kick description of the game, you didn't walk down the aisle with him and agree to all sorts of silly vows so why should you suffer? Eventually exhaustion and very large quantities of beer will take their toll and he will fall into a drunken sleep, no doubt with his pyjamas on inside out and with the same famous tatty scarf, now in need of yet another wash to remove the smell of stale beer, tied round his neck.****

But while his preparations begin weeks in advance, you don't need to do anything until the day before the game. On that morning you will need to pick at your food, refuse to go for a walk and lie in your bed, occasionally sighing. And you will need to maintain that pose until early afternoon when you can stage a minor recovery, involving consumption of small quantities of food, before deteriorating later in the day. And here, my little chums, timing is everything.

You MUST ensure that you wait until it is too late to be taken to the Vet that night; mistime it and not only will you blow your chances of success, but you will find yourself being poked and prodded and having needles stuck into you, for no reason in the world other than to make him and her feel happier and so the Vet can add to the bill.

Secondly, and almost as importantly, your relapse has to be pretty dramatic and a considerable element of over acting has to be involved. Not sure how to over act? Just watch any episode of "Ab Fab" and you'll get the idea.

Timed just right then you can lie in your basket, with your head resting dolefully between your front paws, and watch from the equivalent of a front row seat as the drama unfolds.

"You'll have to take her to the Vet".

"But the Vet will be closed by now".

"I know. I meant tomorrow morning".

"But I'm going to the cup final tomorrow".

"If you phone first thing you can get an early appointment".

"Jim's picking me up at 7".

"You don't have to go with the others. You can take the dog to the Vet and then drive there yourself in plenty of time. The kick off isn't until…when is it?"

"Three o'clock".

"Oh well, you'll have loads of time".

"But Jim lost the draw for who was to be the driver. If I take my own car I won't be able to have a drink".

"Oh so a few pints of beer is more important to you than your dog, is it?"

"No, of course, not".

"Is the match not being shown on the T.V.?"

"Oh aye. It's the Cup Final!".

"Well, that's it sorted. You can take her to the Vet in the morning and then come back and watch the game on the box. I'll even drop in past the supermarket and get you a few cans of beer".

"No. No....it's not the same as being there"

"I know. It will be more comfortable. And you won't get wet. So that's settled then?"

"Well yes, no. Can't you take her? Just this once"

"I'm helping at the "bring and buy" stall at the Church Fair".

"Maybe Maureen could stand in for you".

"She's looking after the jumble stall".

"You could go to the Vet's after the sale".

"The Vet's will be closed by then. So am I to assume that you are happy to let her suffer until Monday?"

And so on. If you watch and listen closely you will witness certain strange phenomena developing. For a start, as his voice gets higher and higher, "he" appears to get smaller. He doesn't of course – what you are witnessing are his knees slowly but surely giving way. By the time he is floundering, desperately trying to find a solution, any solution, that doesn't involve an alteration to his best laid plans, he is actually kneeling on the floor, his hands clasped in a prayer-like manner.

And secondly, the more observant of you will also notice the faintest of smirks appearing on "her" face. In truth the conversation is little more than a charade on her part. She knows how much his day out means to him and she wouldn't want to see him lose out. But at the same time she wants to make him suffer a little if for no other reason than female humans are jealous of the male's ability to, in the blink of an eye, forget all about their responsibility as a husband, father, dog owner, home owner and all that goes with it and become that little boy, out with all the other little boys for a boys' day out.

If you are feeling particularly sadistic, you can let this go on and on until eventually she comes away with "okay I'll get Jill to cover for me at the sale and take her to the Vet". Personally I would be inclined to intervene before then. Slowly emerge from your basket, wagging your tail, and eat a little from your dinner plate. Not too much mind you; you must allow him the opportunity to nip out to the supermarket for "something tasty" for your tea together with a large bag of dog treats.

But in fact such culinary treats are no more than fleeting pleasures, the icing on the cake or, in his case, the icing on the humble pie, and can never come even close to that mental image you have stored away forever of him on his knees with a look on his face that resembles an elderly Bloodhound that has just received some very bad news.

A nice piece of chicken for your tea £2.00. A large bag of rawhide chews £2.50. The image of him begging. Priceless.

*no it's not something you can buy in the Post Office.

**supporters of Aberdeen F.C. will, for obvious reasons, need to think of something else.

***all football players have to have a nickname and one that always ends in a "y".

****based on historic fact circa 11 April, 1970.

# 🐾 TRAIN YOUR 🐾 DOG SITTER

Thought I would finish on a high note with what is not only by far the easiest task to master, but also one of the most rewarding.

I should point out that this chapter will not apply to us all. Sadly there are still dogs out there that spend part of every year behind bars. So what crime have they committed to end up imprisoned? Mugged an old lady in the street to feed their Bonio addiction? No. Spray painted "Dogs Rule" on a building? No. Perhaps been responsible for that most heinous of all crimes, doing a poo in a park, a "crime" that according to our local newspaper should see the reintroduction of capital punishment.

Actually these poor dogs are not guilty of any crime. They are simply saddled with owners who cart them off to Cell block K9 before they themselves head off on holiday.

I covered at some length in "Ask Anna" ways in which you can cure your humans of this terribly selfish trait but for those of you with short memories or for those who didn't buy "Ask Anna" (if not, why not?) here is a brief resume of the salient facts.

1. When you arrive at the kennels refuse to get out of the car so that you have to be dragged out causing the kids to burst into tears.

2. For however long you are in the kennels, sit in a corner with a hang dog look (well when any human is looking anyway – the rest of the time you can please yourself) and be "picky" with your food.

3. When "they" eventually come back for you, crawl out of the kennel as pathetically as caninely possible.

4. When you get home curl up in your basket and refuse to go near even the most appetising food (it's only for another hour or so, so be brave).

5. Wait until the family all agree that you are "never going into kennels again" and just before they phone the Vet, emerge from your basket and eat a little food. The extent of the hugging, kissing and general merriment will assure you that all the suffering was not in vain.

Okay, for dogs who have regularly avoided such confinement or who, courtesy of my advice, will evade such ill treatment in the future, let's get on with the subject of training dog sitters.

First off, you have to understand that the average dog sitter is in total awe of you. After all, they have been given the onerous task of looking after someone else's beloved pet and they are frankly terrified in case they do anything wrong. So you are ahead of the game before the first whistle is sounded. And it is our solemn duty as such treasured creatures to take maximum advantage of that fear in every possible way we can.

I suppose I better tell you a little about my dog sitter. She is a sweet, kind, gentle lady who instantly endeared herself to me the first time we met by arriving at the home with dog treats in her bag. And real quality ones made by a genuine maker of dog foods; not a Poundland bag in sight.

And if that wasn't enough she promptly sat herself down on the floor and allowed me to casually arrange myself across her knee. And it was from this comfortable, if somewhat inelegant pose, that I first noticed that she had something tattooed on her forehead*. The word "sucker".

Her first spell of Anna sitting passed pleasantly if uneventfully and gave me no clue of the joys that would lie ahead. By her second visit, however, I had sussed things out and was all set to exploit her shortcomings i.e. kindness, naivety etc.

For you to fully understand the first part of my plan you need to be aware of a few things that go on in the Gibb household. Like sleeping arrangements for example, which sees "him and her" snoozing away on a fancy memory foam mattress in a large, airy bedroom while I toss and turn and try and get comfy on a lumpy bean bag in the back lobby.

You also need to know that I am not allowed up on the chairs or settees in any of the "public rooms". Oh the "little darlings" can sit on them, stand on them, jump on them, do hand stands on them or whatever they like. There is also no hint of any reprimand if they drop crisps or jammy bread or spill juice on the settee but if I come in and just rest my head on it for a millisecond, I am instantly in the bad books.

Indeed the only piece of furniture that I am allowed to clamber onto is an old sofa in "his" office. When I say "old" I don't mean it is likely to appear on any of the zillions of antique programmes that clog up T.V. these days - you know the ones hosted by Tim Whatatwat, the guy with the garish bow ties and a gap between his front teeth, or one of the many other pillocks who drone on and on in reverent terms about something the average human wouldn't give house room to. No I mean "old" in the sense that it has seen better days; except in this case it is more a case of having seen better years and even decades.

Still it is comfy and it is mine and I can stretch out in total contentment. But only during the day. For some reason known only to "him and her", when night time comes around I am not allowed to lie there and be comfortable. Oh no. I am packed off to the back lobby and, yes, that lumpy bean bag.

I do try every so often to refuse to go to my bed, ready to sneak upstairs when their backs are turned, but without success. He simply hooks a finger under my collar and drags me to my bed, oblivious to the damage he could be doing to my carefully manicured claws.

And that is where the joy of having a Dog Sitter (DS from now on) starts to show itself. I must be honest the first time I tried the old "I don't want to go to my bed" routine with mine

I had little hope of success. I assumed she would simply follow his example and man handle, or in her case woman handle, me to my bed. But no. What happened in fact is that she sat down beside me and began to "reason with me".

Oh how I wish somebody could have recorded that moment - I am sure it would have been a big hit on Youtube. This caring lady sitting for ages trying to explain to me why I had to go to my bed and how "mum and dad would be annoyed" if I didn't. Oh come on, dear. By that time of night "they" were probably out of it on their second bottle of cheap plonk and had no doubt forgotten they even had a dog let alone be concerned whether I slept in my own bed, the upstairs sofa or even the roof.

Eventually my poor DS admitted defeat and headed off to her own bed leaving me lying with that pathetic look that I have mastered over the years. So I gave it five minutes and then tiptoed up the stairs to a sofa with my name on it**.

The second night the "pep" talk lasted only about 10 minutes before she gave up and I headed upstairs and by night three she had realised that it had been a battle of wills and that she had clearly lost. Round one to me.

The next time that my DS came to stay the sleeping arrangements were already set in stone and she put up no argument, realising it was fruitless, and simply went along with my wishes. It was at that point that I decided we needed to up the stakes.

As I have explained elsewhere in this book, my morning toilet arrangements are totally dictated by him and her. If they decide to get up early I get out early; if they decide to have a lie in, sadly so do I. Now I'm an early waker. By 5 a.m. most days I am bright eyed and bushy tailed and have got seriously stuck into the morning task of cleaning my nether regions. Let's face it, trapped in a back lobby with a lumpy bean bag for company, there isn't much else to do. And by that stage of the day, I would rather welcome the opportunity to pay a "visit to the rest room" as our strange Transatlantic cousins like to describe having a pee.

I still remember the morning I had my Eureka moment. As I lay there, stretched out on my old sofa, I kept thinking to myself "it couldn't work could it? Could she really be that much of a soft touch?". Eventually I came to the conclusion that there was only one way of finding out. So I trooped downstairs and was delighted to find the door to the bedroom, where my DS was sleeping, slightly ajar. I was into the room like a shot, rested my rather attractive head on the bed covers and waited.

I didn't have to wait long. As soon as my sad, pitiful eyes locked with her "sleepy quickly turned to panic" eyes, she dived out of her bed in a manner that Tom Daley would have been proud of, clearly alarmed in case there was something wrong with me. Before I even had the opportunity of pointing her in the right direction, the front door was opened and my own private loo awaited me. And as I wandered around the grass looking for a suitable spot, I did feel mildly guilty about the forlorn creature shivering in her nightie at the front door. But only mildly.

The early morning "toilet break" all too soon became a daily routine and left me wondering "what's next?" After all I had my poor DS on the run so there was no point in giving up was there? How about an early breakfast? So waiting until my friend was settled back in her bed I paid her a another visit, anticipating she would again leap out of bed and quickly fill my bowl with Butcher's best tripe. I was therefore more than a little taken aback when she failed to rise to my bait, or even rise out of her bed, and instead politely but firmly informed me that it "wasn't breakfast time" yet.

Whoa! What was going on? Didn't she understand the Dog Sitter/ Dog relationship? But then it dawned on me; this was all "his" doing. He may have been a long way off but his evil hand was still firmly on the controls. Clearly he had left strict instructions about my feeding times and the DS was scared to deviate from them. So I returned to the lobby and lay down with a long, audible sigh. Twenty minutes later I reappeared in the bedroom to be greeted by the same dismissive comment.

For the next hour the battle of wills continued. I pulled out all the stops – laying my head on the bed covers close to her face, the pathetic whimper, the tail wagging (which for some reason humans seem to be particularly susceptible to) and so on. Until eventually I simply wore her down. And then like music to my ears, I heard the magic words "all right, come on and I'll get you your breakfast".

Game, set and match to me I believe.

Sadly all too soon my humans came back home, looking like a pair of Halloween cakes and armed with hundreds and hundreds of photographs which they insisted on showing to everyone – "oh here's one of me on our hotel balcony and here's one of her on the balcony and here's one of both of us the balcony taken with the camera timer and...." Well you get the idea.

Initially I thought that I had just been particularly fortunate with my allotted Dog Sitter but subsequent events, when "him and her" decided to jet off to London, proved that wasn't the case. I don't know much about London never having been taken there, unlike one of my predecessors. My late pal Lucy told me that the even later Heather the Westie had been taken by them to London. Mind you Heather ended up piddling in Hamley's Toy Shop so perhaps that's the reason that subsequent visits by him and her to London have been devoid of canine companionship.

I have heard of lots of reasons for going to London from the sensible (to watch the greyhound racing at the Wimbledon Stadium) to the ridiculous (to stand in the rain waving a silly little flag as the son of that chinless wonder – you know the one whose Mother wears loads of bling on her head and lives in that huge Palace - gets married) but "hers" truly takes the biscuit.

You'll honestly never guess why she went. Okay if you'll never guess I might as well tell you. She went all the way to

London to look at flowers. I know, I know. She could have taken me for a walk round the neighbourhood and stared at all the gardens or better still gone for a meander round one of our local parks. Instead she goes all the way to London and spends a whole Saturday doing nothing but wandering from one plant to another.

And she paid for the privilege as well. Honestly, I'm not making this up. And while I don't know how much it cost, by the way "he" spoke about it (with tears running down his face) I can only assume that it was a LOT.

Anyway when they headed off to London I was dumped at the caravan in Perthshire with a stand in "him and her" who fortunately turned out to be just as nice to me as my regular Dog Sitter. Which was pretty surprising when you consider that the "her" wasn't even a dog fan. Mind you my charm quickly won her round and caused her to revise her opinion of the canine race. Okay she's not likely to head off to Crufts anytime soon but at least she's a lot happier in the company of us dogs than she was before she met me.

And we all had a pleasant few days at the caravan helped in no small measure by the fact that the weather was glorious – the best week of the whole year and my owners missed it. How can you tell I'm smirking?

What was also great fun was being able to walk where I wanted to go. I am sure you all know the feeling when you are out for a walk on the lead of deciding you would like to go in a certain direction, one that deviates from that chosen by your owner, and him making it abundantly clear that "he" is in charge. Problem is "he" is stronger than me and when my claws being dragged across tarmac start to emit sparks, I am forced to admit that I have no option but to go with him. Not so with my temporary DS. I was in command and he just followed me where ever I wanted to go. At last I knew the meaning of the phrase "taking your human for a walk".

It was during that week at the caravan that I reached the conclusion that all Dog Sitters have one thing in common; they are all push-overs.

So when you are left with a Dog Sitter make the best of your opportunity. Just remember a Dog Sitter is not for life just for the holidays.


*No not literally. Please don't wander about staring at the foreheads of every woman you pass in the street

**Again, not literally. It just means ...oh forget it.

# Dogs should show restraint

"for goodness sake, at least wait until they get in the car!"

## Dogs should always listen properly

"See. Told you I was clever. My human's taking me to be tutored"

## WHAT IS FRIENDS OF BIANCA?

Friends of Bianca is a registered Scottish charity (SCO42783) founded to provide desperately needed support for a shelter for severely abused and neglected dogs and cats in Portugal. (www.friendsofbianca.org). The idea to start Friends of Bianca came when Mike was on holiday in Portugal and was horrified, not only by the sheer number of stray and abandoned animals wandering around, but the condition they were in.

Friends of Bianca was registered as a charity in December 2011 and in its first twelve months raised over £12500 for the shelter in Portugal while incurring a mere £159 in expenditure, meaning that 99% of all monies donated went directly to animal care. The money raised has been utilised to undertake capital projects that Bianca would otherwise have been unable to finance. This has included the replacement of the existing fenced enclosure with a new block and metal plate external wall, not only making the shelter safer for the animals but allowing it to be extended to house more animals in desperate need of care.

Friends of Bianca are currently endeavouring to raise the money to complete the building and equipping of an on site medical clinic facility (one that will enable the shelter volunteers to carry out minor procedures without costly and time consuming visits to a Vet) and a "mother and puppy" enclosure that will provide the young dogs with both suitable housing and a puppy only exercise area. Other projects to improve the shelter, and the lives of the animals in their care, are also in the pipeline.

## WHAT IS BIANCA?

Bianca Associacao is a Portuguese charity, run solely by volunteers, which annually rescues, cares for and re-homes, some 600 abandoned dogs and cats, many arriving in terrible condition. In the absence of a rescue shelter in the Sesimbra area of Portugal run by any of the National animal welfare societies, many poor creatures would undoubtedly starve or suffer a painful death from treatable injuries or diseases if they weren't rescued by Bianca

Bianca is run exclusively by unpaid volunteers with NO paid administration staff.

At any one time the shelter accommodates over 300 dogs with a further 30 cats being looked after in foster homes. Where street cats cannot be accommodated, the shelter pays for the animals to be spayed and neutered and in 2012 some 803 animals were helped in some way by the charity.

Bianca regularly works with the local community especially the school children, teaching them about animal care, while a number of the children attend the shelter regularly to socialise and exercise the dogs.

Through a network of contacts, a substantial proportion of the dogs which come into Bianca's care are re-homed around Europe with large numbers going to new homes in the likes of Germany, The Netherlands, Sweden, Denmark and many other European countries.

In 2014 Friends of Bianca hope that they will be able to start bringing dogs from the shelter to new homes in North East of Scotland.

To learn more about Bianca's remarkable work, go to the web site at www.bianca.pt/english

## HOW CAN I HELP?

### By becoming a God Parent

Although Bianca re-home a large number of animals every year, there are certain animals that sadly will never find homes and that will remain in the care of the charity for life – no healthy animal is ever put to sleep. Currently 200 animals fall into that category and you can become a God Parent to one of them for a mere £2.50/ 3 Euros/ $4.00 a month. Your name will appear on your chosen animal's web page and you will receive a personalised certificate with a photo of the dog or cat. To see the animals looking for sponsors go to www.bianca.pt/english and scroll down to "Animals For Fostering"; once you have chosen an animal (or animals) send details to our Fostering Co-ordinator Heather McBride at hjmcbride@sympatico.ca and she will do the rest.

### By volunteering

We are always delighted to hear from anyone who might like to help in anyway with our fund raising efforts, so if it interests you, contact Mike at info@friendsofbianca.org or on 07903 463163. While much of our fund raising is conducted in and around Aberdeen, we have a number of volunteers in Canada, the USA and The Netherlands who fund raise in their own back yard. So if you have an idea of how you can help Friends of Bianca please get in touch.

Or why not spend a few days in beautiful Portugal helping with the animals at the shelter, which is close to the wonderful city of Lisbon and to the beaches? There are regular flights from many cities, including Edinburgh, to Lisbon Airport where you would be met by a volunteer from the shelter. Modestly priced en suite accommodation (roughly 25 Euros a night) is available at the Casa de Maria guest house near the shelter and the Bianca group regularly organise social evenings, barbecues and the like for visiting volunteers. If you would like to find out more about volunteering contact Mike.

**AND FINALLY**

If you would like to be kept up to date with news of Friends of Bianca's work then email the charity and we will send you our regular online newsletter.(info@friendsofbianca.org).

## SINCERE THANKS ARE DUE TO:

### DAVID STOUT of Sketchpad

David not only designed the brilliant cover, but also provided all the art work for the cartoons, adverts, recipe pages and the like.

### MICHELLE McMANUS

Anna and Mike met Michelle on The Hour in 2009 when Anna marked her first time in a T.V. studio by clearing several glasses of water from a coffee table with a single swish of her tail leaving the floor of the studio wet and strewn with glass, a mere five minutes before the show went out live! Despite that, Michelle kindly agreed to write a foreword to this book.

### HEATHER McBRIDE

Heather not only supplied all the "Bernie" recipes but also proof read the book (so if you find any errors you now know who to blame!)

### ALL AT THE BIANCA SHELTER

For providing the background to the amazing "Stories from the Shelter" and for all the fantastic work they do.

### NORMA GIBB

The butt for so many jokes, comments and general dogs abuse in this book, all taken with such good grace (we hope!). Anna and Mike both know how fortunate they are to share their lives with "her indoors".

**Artist Profile**

**Lily Taylor**

*After leaving school and college where I won awards for Art, the ability lay dormant for some time until I worked at Aberdeen University and trained as a cartographer. This led me to be asked to illustrate, in Pen and Ink, an ornithologists' quarterly report after studying the Birds in their natural habitat.*

*After a gap of some more years, I joined an art class where I was introduced to pastels amongst other media. This is now my medium choice and all paintings shown on my website are in Pastel unless stated otherwise. I have subsequently taken the opportunity to study under two of Scotlands' best pastellists' Margaret Evans and Fiona Haldane. I still travel to training courses and workshops run by other artists as I feel technique can be applied to any medium and currently attend two art classes in Aberdeen run by two other well known Scottish artists.*

*My favourite subject is Animals but particularly Dogs which I have owned and shown for over 30 years having bred champions and judged all over the country, so feel I know my subject well. I travel to Africa frequentl y to visit my family and photograph Wildlife there to reproduce in my art. My work has hung in The Milton Gallery, Country Frames Gallery, Hennies Gallery and am delighted to have exhibited at the Pitlochry Theatre Gallery this Spring. I have entered and sold work through other Exhibitions and as part of various Art Clubs/Societies where I am a member.*

*I undertake many Commissions on Pets and animals and this is my most enjoyable work. Capturing the expression of an owners' pet in a piece of work then seeing their reaction on viewing the finished work is a privilege.*

*I can be contacted through the following for advice or further information:-*

www.lilytaylorart.com

email: lilytaylorart@hotmail.co.uk

Tel: 01224 680702 or 07774 712589

118